DISCARD

Measuring at the Fire Station

Dianne Irving

Real World Math Books are published by Capstone Press,
151 Good Counsel Drive, P.O. Box 669, Mankato, Minnesota 56002.
www.capstonepress.com

Copyright © 2010 by Capstone Press, a Capstone imprint.
All rights reserved.
No part of this publication may be reproduced in whole or in part, or stored in a retrieval system, or transmitted in any form or by any means, electronic, mechanical, photocopying, recording, or otherwise, without written permission of the publisher.
For information regarding permission, write to Capstone Press,
151 Good Counsel Drive, P.O. Box 669, Dept. R, Mankato, Minnesota 56002.
Printed in the United States of America in Stevens Point, Wisconsin.

122009
005647WZS10

Books published by Capstone Press are manufactured with paper containing at least 10 percent post-consumer waste.

Library of Congress Cataloging-in-Publication Data
Irving, Dianne.
  Measuring at the fire station / by Dianne Irving. -- 1st hardcover ed.
    p. cm. -- (Real world math)
  Includes index.
  ISBN 978-1-4296-5190-5 (lib. bdg.)
 1. Fire engines--Juvenile literature. 2. Measurement--Juvenile literature. 3. Problem solving--Juvenile literature. I. Title. II. Series.

TH9372.I78 2009
628.9′25--dc22

2009051383

Editorial Credits
Sara Johnson, editor; Emily R. Smith, M.A.Ed., editorial director; Sharon Coan, M.S.Ed., editor-in-chief; Lee Aucoin, creative director; Rachelle Cracchiolo, M.S.Ed., publisher

Photo Credits
The author and publisher would like to gratefully credit or acknowledge the following for permission to reproduce copyright material: cover Photolibrary; p.1 Photos.com; p.4 Alamy; p.5 Getty Images; p.6 Getty Images; p.7 Alamy; p.8 Mary Evans Picture Library; p.9 Mary Evans Picture Library; p.10 Bigstock/© Scrappin Stacey; p.11 Alamy; p.12 Corbis; p.13 (top) Mary Evans Picture Library; p.13 (bottom) Bigstock/© Judy 823; p.14 Getty Images; p.15 Getty Images; p.16 Photos.com; p.17 Bigstock/© Kalliope; p.18 Bigstock/© Sonyae; p.19 Bigstock/© C.J. Cornell; p.20 Getty Images; p.21 Photos.com; p.22 Alamy; p.23 Photolibrary; p.24 Getty Images; p.25 Getty Images; p.26 Getty Images; p.27 Getty Images; p.28 Shutterstock; p.29 Bigstock/© Joy R

While every care has been taken to trace and acknowledge copyright, the publishers tender their apologies for any accidental infringement where copyright has proved untraceable. They would be pleased to come to a suitable arrangement with the rightful owner in each case.

Table of Contents

A Field Trip	4
Before Fire Engines	6
Early Fire Engines	8
Motorized Fire Vehicles	14
Fire Engines Today	16
Firefighters	22
Problem-Solving Activity	28
Glossary	30
Index	31
Internet Sites	31
Answer Key	32

A Field Trip

Today we went on a field trip to the fire station. We met some firefighters. We learned so much about fire engines and firefighters!

The fire engines are kept at the fire station.

The First Fire Brigade

The first fire **brigade** (brih-GADE) was in **ancient** Rome. They put buckets of water on the ends of poles and tipped them on a fire.

A fire engine is not just another name for a fire truck. A fire engine carries its own water supply. It pumps water onto a fire. A fire truck may not carry water to a fire.

A fire engine carries a large **volume** of water. It can carry 1,000 gallons (3,785.4 L) of water to a fire.

Before Fire Engines

Before fire engines, water was carried to a fire in buckets. Each bucket carried about 3 gallons (11.4 L) of water. The water was thrown onto the fire.

Fire Safety

Long ago, there was a law that said every house in America had to keep a bucket of water on the front steps. If there was a fire, everybody would grab their buckets and help put out the fire.

Later, firefighters used carts that carried large tanks of water. These were pulled by the firefighters.

LET'S EXPLORE MATH

Some old water tanks held 90 gallons (340.6 L) of water. Firefighters used buckets to get the water from the tanks. Each bucket held about 3 gallons (11.4 L) of water. How many buckets of water could be taken from a 90-gallon (340.6 L) tank?

Early Fire Engines

The first fire engines had water tanks and pumps. Firefighters had to work together to pump the handles up and down by hand.

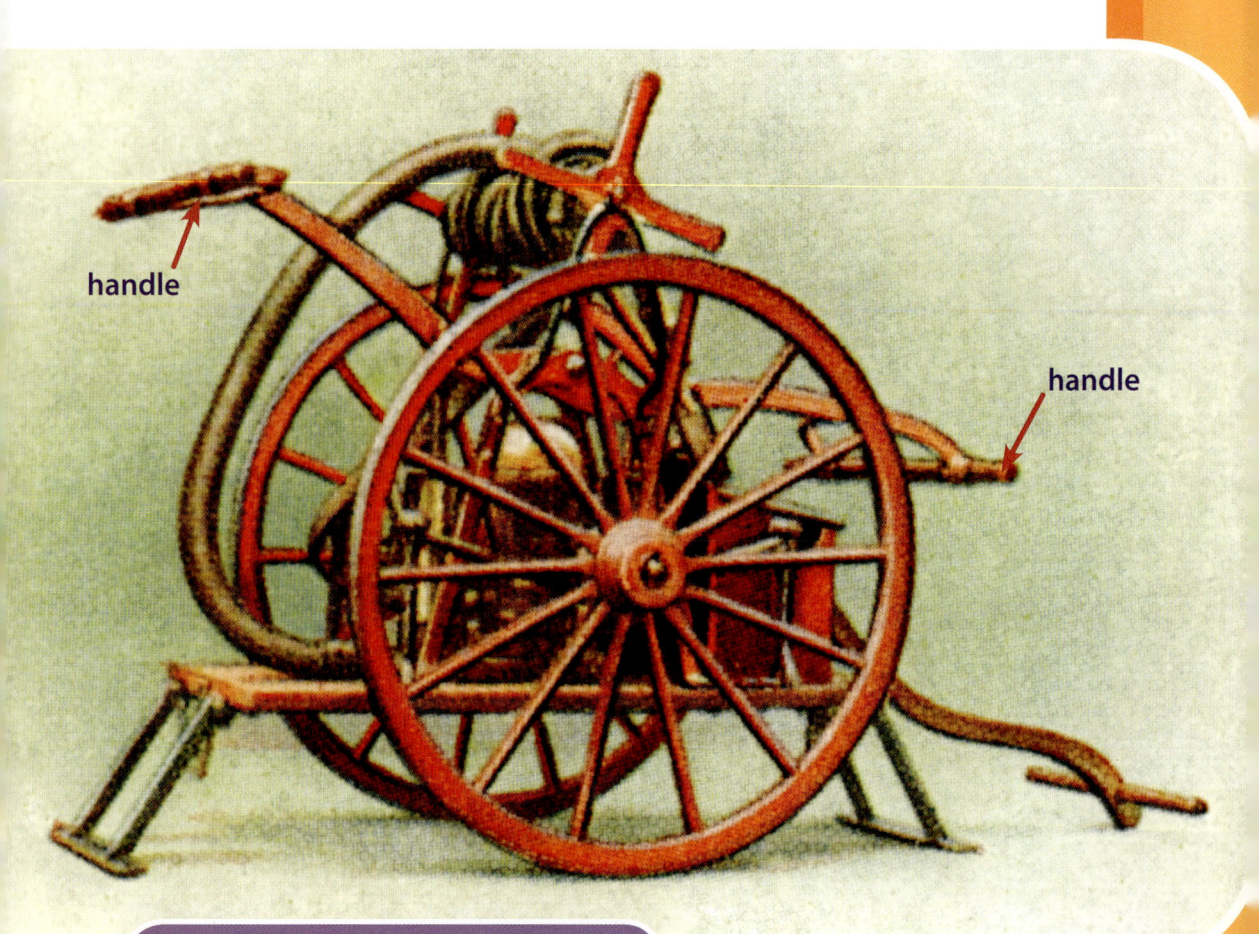

handle

handle

This fire engine was built in 1870.

Firefighters pumped the handles 60 times a minute. It was hard work! The water could travel up to 180 feet (54.8 m) from the end of the hose onto a fire.

LET'S EXPLORE MATH

Firefighters could pump the water a length of 180 feet (54.8 m) to put out a fire.

a. How far would the water have to travel if the fire was only half that length away?

b. How much farther does the water need to travel if it has traveled 60 feet and the fire is 180 feet away?

Hoses were carried on separate **vehicles** (VEE-hih-kuhlz). Some hose carts carried about 400 feet (122 m) of hose.

Measuring Length

In the United States, the "foot" is a unit used to measure length. Other units used to measure length are inches, yards, and miles.

1 inch
12 inches = 1 foot
3 feet = 1 yard
1,760 yards = 1 mile

Later fire engines had steam engines to work the pumps. Steam pushed the water through hoses.

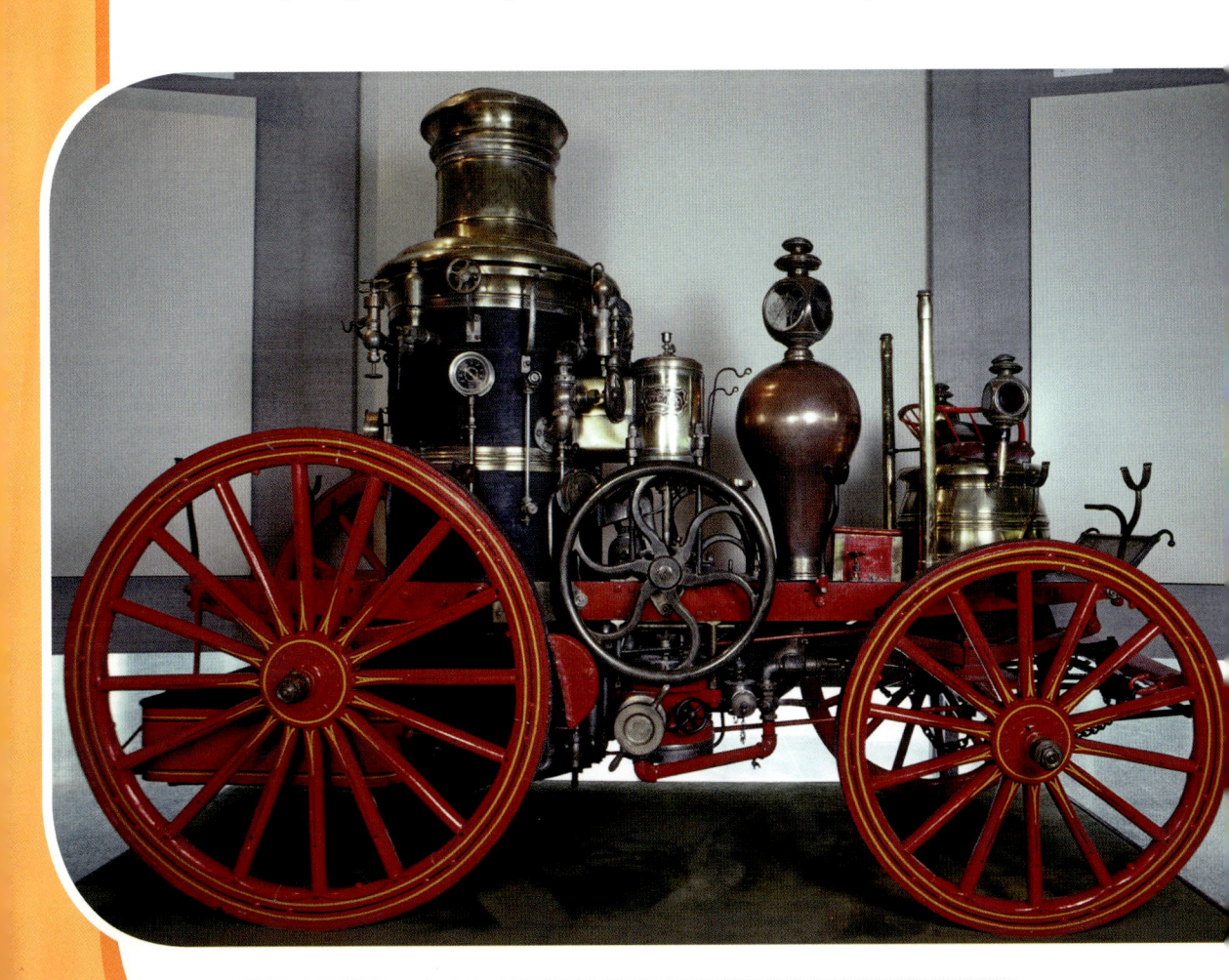

Safer Engines

The old, hand-pumped fire engines had to be dangerously close to a fire. Because steam fire engines could pump water farther, the firefighters could stay a safer distance from the fires.

Steam fire engines could pump water at 700 gallons (2,650 L) per minute. Water could go 200 feet (61 m) high and 300 feet (91.4 m) **horizontally** (hor-uh-ZAHN-tuh-lee).

LET'S EXPLORE MATH

Water from a steam fire engine could reach 200 feet in the air.

a. If a building is 10 stories high and each story is 12 feet high, how high is the building?

b. How many feet above the building could be reached by water from a steam fire engine?

Some of these steam fire engines weighed over 5,000 pounds (2,268 kg). They were pulled by horses. They were too heavy to be pulled by men.

Guard Dogs

Most fire stations had dalmatian dogs to protect the horses while they were inside the fire stations or at fires. This is why dalmatians are often the symbols of fire stations!

Motorized Fire Vehicles

In the early 1900s, motors were put in fire engines. This meant horses did not have to pull the heavy engines anymore.

So Long!

Many people were sad to see the fire horses go. In 1922, about 50,000 people gathered to say goodbye to the Detroit Fire Department horses.

A **motorized** (MO-tuh-rizd) fire engine could carry a lot. It carried the pump, tank, and hoses.

Motorized fire engines could carry all the tools needed to fight a fire.

Fire Engines Today

Today, fire engines carry hoses and ladders. They also carry other tools to the fires. They have pumps and water tanks.

Modern fire engines weigh about 37,000 pounds (16,783 kg). That's more than 7 times the weight of early fire engines. Luckily, firefighters do not have to pull them!

LET'S EXPLORE MATH

In the past, fire engines weighed about 5,000 pounds.

a. How many pounds would 3 fire engines weigh altogether?

b. How many fire engines would there be at a fire if the engines weigh 25,000 pounds altogether?

Fire engines are about 27 feet 2 inches (8.3 m) long. That is almost the same length as 2 small family cars.

The United States has over 68,000 fire engines that pump water onto fires.

Not Always Red

Most fire engines in the United States are red. But sometimes they are yellow, white, or even dark blue!

The tanks in modern fire engines carry at least 1,000 gallons (3,785.4 L) of water. Water can be pumped out at 800 gallons (3,028.3 L) per minute.

Firefighters may need more water than a fire engine can hold. So they use **fire hydrants** to help them keep fighting the fire.

Drink Up

If you drink 8 glasses of water a day, it would take you more than 5 years to drink all the water in a fire engine tank.

Fire engines can pump water from fire hydrants and other water supplies. There are also smaller fire trucks that do not carry water tanks. These fire trucks also pump water from the fire hydrants.

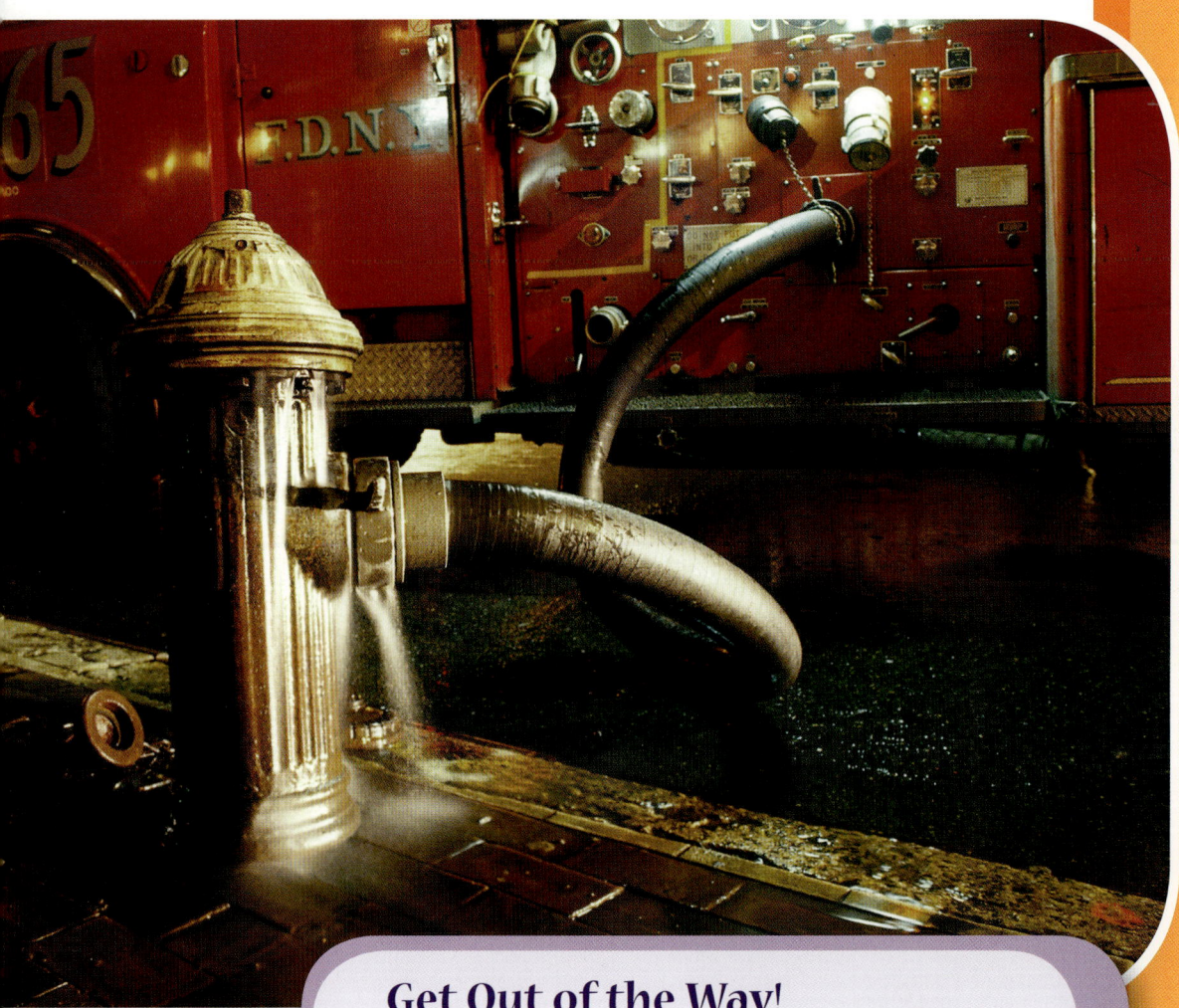

Get Out of the Way!

Fire engines can pump water so fast that the water would knock you down! Hoses must be held by at least 2 firefighters.

Fire engines carry more than 1,400 feet (426.7 m) of hoses. That is nearly the same length as 4 football fields.

LET'S EXPLORE MATH

Fire hoses are very heavy. A hose weighs about 1 pound (0.45 kg) for every 4 feet (1.2 m) of hose.

a. If the hose is 40 feet long, how much does it weigh?

b. If the hose weighs 50 pounds, how long is it?

Firefighters

Fire engines are kept in fire stations. Fire stations also have places for firefighters to sleep and eat. Firefighters do a lot of waiting.

Somewhere in the United States, a fire station alarm rings every 20 seconds!

When somebody reports a fire, the fire alarm in the station rings. Firefighters must get ready very quickly.

Firefighters must put on their special clothes and boots. Full firefighting gear is very heavy to wear.

This firefighter is dressed in the gear worn to fight fires.

LET'S EXPLORE MATH

Full firefighting gear weighs about 100 pounds (45.4 kg). If the average weight of a firefighter is 180 pounds (81.6 kg), what is the total weight of 2 firefighters and their gear?

When firefighters hear the fire alarm, they are ready to leave in 90 seconds or less. That is fast!

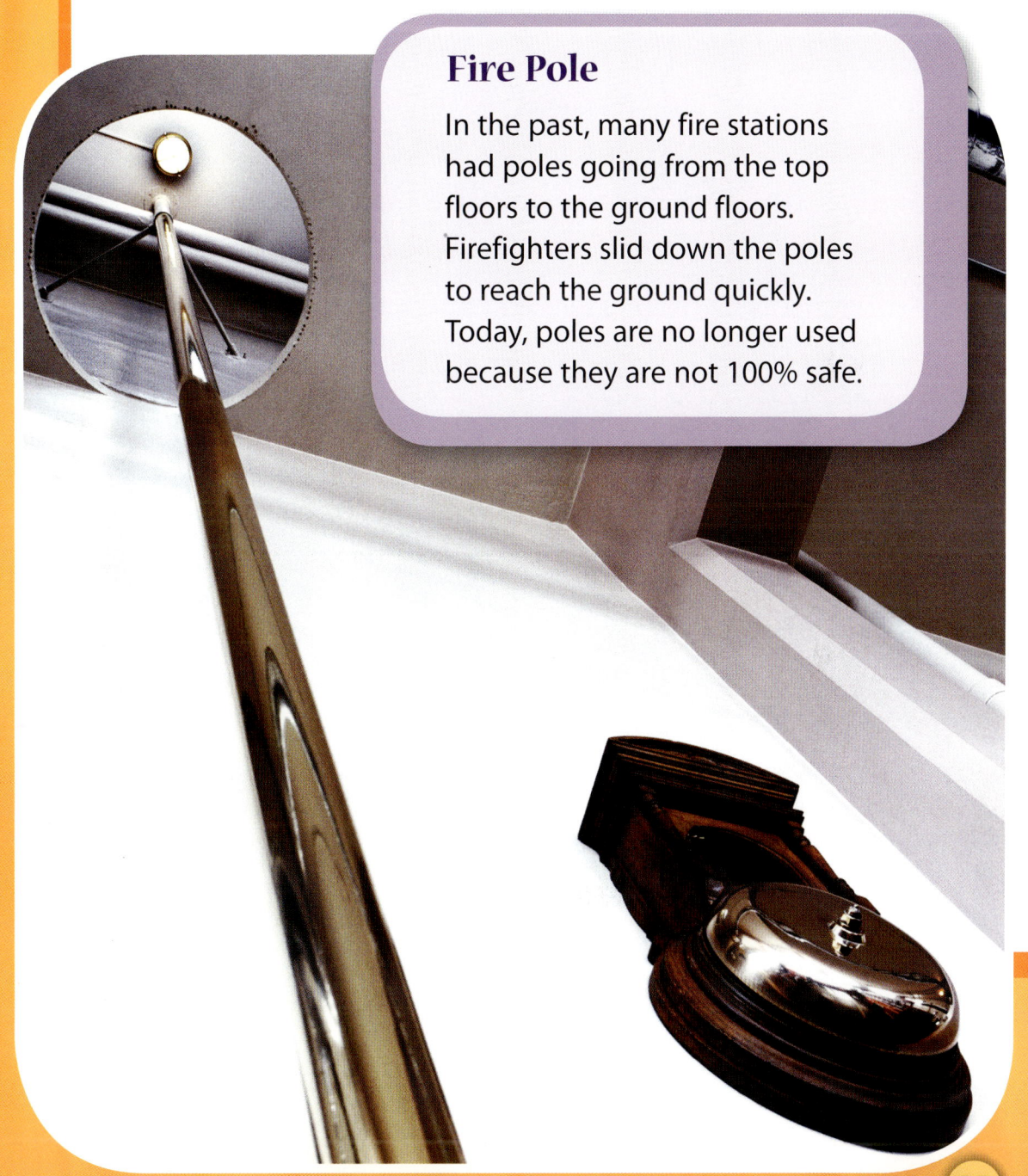

Fire Pole

In the past, many fire stations had poles going from the top floors to the ground floors. Firefighters slid down the poles to reach the ground quickly. Today, poles are no longer used because they are not 100% safe.

It must be very hard work to be a firefighter. But they have lots of great tools to help them.

Emergency 911

If you need to report a fire, call 9-1-1.

I loved visiting the fire station. When I grow up, I am going to be a firefighter. I wonder what fire engines will be like then.

Problem-Solving Activity

Hosing Down the Problem

Edwina's house is rectangular. It is 33 feet (10 m) wide and 50 feet (15 m) long. There is a faucet at the front left-hand corner of her house. She wants to plant a garden around the **perimeter** of her house.

Solve It!

a. What is the total length around Edwina's garden?

b. How long would Edwina's hose need to be to water all of her garden?

Hint: She needs to follow the edge of the garden. She can carry the hose either left or right from the faucet.

Use the steps on page 29 to help you solve the problems.

Step 1: Draw a plan of Edwina's house. Draw a faucet at the front left-hand corner. Label the length and width of each side of the house in feet.

Step 2: Add up the lengths and widths of Edwina's house to find the perimeter.

Step 3: Find the part of the garden that is farthest away from the faucet.

Step 4: Add the side lengths to find the distance from the faucet to the farthest part of the garden. This is how long the hose would need to be.

Glossary

ancient—very old

brigade—a group of people organized for a special activity

fire hydrants—outlets connected to the main water supply from which firefighters can get water

horizontally—level to the horizon; the horizon is the line where the land and the sky meet.

modern—up-to-date, relating to the present

motorized—having a motor or an engine

perimeter—the distance around a shape

vehicles—machines that carry or transport something

volume—the amount of space something takes up

Index

cart, 7, 10

feet, 9, 10, 12, 18, 21, 28, 29

fire brigade, 4

fire engine, 4–5, 6, 8–21, 22, 27

firefighter, 4, 7, 8–9, 11, 17, 20, 22–27

fire hydrant, 19–20

fire station, 4, 13, 22–23, 25

fire truck, 5, 20

gallon, 5, 6, 7, 12 19

horses, 13, 14

hose, 10–11, 15, 16, 20–21, 28, 29

kilograms, 13, 17, 21, 24

ladder, 16

liter, 5, 6, 7, 12, 19

meter, 9, 10, 12, 18, 21, 28, 29

pounds, 13, 17, 21, 24

pump, 5, 8–9, 11–12, 15, 16, 19–20

tank, 7, 8, 15, 16, 19, 20

volume, 5

water, 4–5, 6–7, 8–9, 11–12, 16, 18–20, 28

yard, 10

Internet Sites

FactHound offers a safe, fun way to find Internet sites related to this book. All of the sites on FactHound have been researched by our staff.

Here's all you do:

Visit *www.facthound.com*

FactHound will fetch the best sites for you!

31

Answer Key

Let's Explore Math

Page 7:
Amount of water in tank ÷ amount of water in each bucket = number of buckets
90 gallons ÷ 3 gallons = 30 buckets

Page 9:
a. 180 feet ÷ 2 = 90 feet (27.4 m)
b. 180 feet – 60 feet = 120 feet (36.5 m) left to travel

Page 12:
a. 10 stories × 12 feet = 120 feet
b. 200 feet – 120 feet = 80 feet above the building could be reached by the water.

Page 17:
a. 5,000 pounds x 3 = 15,000 pounds altogether
b. 25,000 pounds ÷ 5,000 pounds = 5 fire engines

Page 21:
a. 40 feet ÷ 4 = 10 pounds
b. 50 pounds × 4 = 200 feet

Page 24:
100 pounds + 180 pounds = 280 pounds per firefighter
280 + 280 = 560 pounds

Problem-Solving Activity

a. The total length of Edwina's garden would be
33 feet + 50 feet + 33 feet + 50 feet = 166 feet.
b. Edwina's hose would need to be 33 feet + 50 feet = 83 feet long.